The Making of a Socialist
(LE DOCUMENT HUMAINE)

BY
Rev. ROLAND D. SAWYER

The Making of a Socialist

(LE DOCUMENT HUMAINE)

BY

Rev. ROLAND D. SAWYER

———

"There is no life of a man, faithfully recorded, but is an heroic poem of its sort, rhymed or un-rhymed." *Carlyle.*

———

PUBLISHED BY THE ARIEL PRESS
WESTWOOD, MASS.

ISBN: 978-1-6673-0519-6 paperback
ISBN: 978-1-6673-0520-2 hardcover

*To My Comrades
In the Great International
Socialist Movement,
I Dedicate
This Little Account of
How I came to be one with
them.*

INTRODUCTION

I have written out here in these seven chapters how I was made a Socialist, and how I feel now I am one. I have not had much of a public or official life, but I have lived my personal life very intensive, it has all been very sweet to me, very interesting; and in putting it in black and white, I have acted on Wendell Phillip's suggestion, that a man interested in himself is interesting to other men. For nearly twenty years, since my break in health and leaving the bench, I have lived most largely in the intellectual life of my time, so far as able, by my reading, study, contact with men. I am as deeply persuaded as I can be, by the result of this twenty years effort, that Socialism is the great living movement of the age. I hope that my showing of this in these chapters may be of help to some workingmen and women who cannot find themselves able to leave the bench to study as I have done.

If my little story of my life can serve to strengthen the conviction of any working man or woman that Socialism is the way out of bondage for them, their family and their class; or if it can arouse any working man or woman to see this, then my effort will be repaid, and I shall feel warranted in having taken time and space to tell the story.   For I was to the working class born; my ancestors were early here in America to battle with the harsh environments and wrench a living from the soil, they carry in their physique the marks of the toilers. I am proud of them as having ever been of the great class that pays its way, that carries the burden of the world. I am a class-conscious workingman; I am with my class; I battle *for* them, and all I ask is, that they will arouse themselves, so that I may battle *with* them.

As the story of a working man, who by force of circumstances was forced from the bench, to give his time to reading and study, and thus to see things a little more intelligently than many of the workers have opportunity to do, I want this sketch of my life to be considered.

I have ventured to have this story published for several reasons: one is, that several who read it in the New York Call have written to me suggesting such a course; another is, that while we have built up a good scientific literature of Socialism here in America, yet we are short of books of lighter vein, biography, fiction, poetry: "mere literature" with us is scant, sol feel there is a place for such a book; again I don't know why the story is not well enuf told to be put into a book; but the reason above all others is, that my faith in the Cause is such, that I would rather my name be permanently connected with it than with anything else.

The "Making of My Socialism" I consider the most important thing in my life; for the Cause, I have thrown away any chances I may have had of professional success; I have sacrificed many things that once loomed big for me, and thus I want to put on record my affiliation with the International Socialist Movement.

ROLAND D. SAWYER

Ware, Mass. Oct. 1911.

CHAPTER I

THE SHOEMAKER'S CHILD

"Ho! workers of the old time, styled
  The Gentle Craft of Leather!
Young brothers of an ancient guild, —
  Stand forth once more together."
                Whittier's Shoemakers.

CHAPTER I

———

THE SHOEMAKER'S CHILD

———

WAS born at Kensington about 1 P. M., January 8, 1874, in the little white cottage near the East School house, now the residence of Daniel Worthen and his wife. My parents at the time rented this cottage from Abigail Chase, who was present at my birth. Like Mirabeau, the first comment my appearance on this planet excited was caused by my physical appearance, for Miss Chase exclaimed: "See what a long fellow he is." There are five things that interest me, absorb me, now I have reached mature life; they are the love of Nature, thirst for knowledge, domestic affections, religion, and the desire to help humanity, which can best be done thru Socialism. All of these save the last were at least embryonately present that first day of my embarking upon the voyage of life.

Back of the cottage stretched away for many rods a rugged piece of New Hampshire ledge, which was crowned by a splendid growth of pines. In front of the cottage was a fine grove of great oaks. The first sound that must have greeted my ears, tho I don't remember it, would be the soughing of the pines, and the roar of the oaks in the New England snow storm that was raging. How could one but grow to be a nature lover when she greeted his advent with such manifestations of her grandeur? How could one but come to love the murmur of the pines as Emerson did, or the roar of the naked oaks as did Burns?

The next sound that must have reached my ears was the ringing of the teacher's bell at the East school, a few rods away, as it summoned the children to take up the task of acquiring knowledge. I think this must have inspired me with the desire to know things, to read, the love of books, etc.; anyhow, I don't remember where that desire began if it did not begin then. And then I was taken to the breast of my mother, and from her caresses and the love of the parents, I developed, as the race has developed, those natural affections, which have ever been such a source of satisfaction to me.

As for religion, why, religion had been the chief concern of people in New England for 250 years, and of course, a religious inclination must have been passed down to me. And anyway, as Sabbatier says, "Man is an incorrigibly religious animal," so We are made up with the spark of religion in us, it only awaits to be fanned into a flame in later life. Thus the only new thing that I have developed is my Socialism, and in these columns I am going to tell how the others grew, and how this new thing developed.

My father's family descended from William Sawyer, one of the early settlers at old Newbury, Mass. What William Sawyer looked like I cannot say, but the typical Sawyer stature, so far back as I know it, is a short, thickish man with large hands and feet, a stature that evidently indicates that the Sawyers have for a long time been among the "hewers of wood and drawers of water."

Their physical make-up puts them into the ranks of the toilers, a family of that great class that has carried the burdens of the world.

Beetfild Sawyer was an ancestor who left the West Newbury family about 1800, to settle in the town of Hill, about 40 miles above Concord.

After various struggles to gain a living, his descendants for the most part drifted down toward the Massachusetts line, among them being my grandfather Calvin, who had located first in Plaistow, and later in Kensington.

My mother's family, the Blakes, was one of the early families to settle in the important settlement of Hampton, from which township Kensington was later set off. The prevailing physical type among the Blakes seems to have been a tall stature, slender in earlier years, but developing stoutness as the years go by.

In the marriage of my grandfather and grandmother, the Blake blood mingled with that of another old Hampton family, the Moultons. These Moultons were physically a fine type of Anglo-Saxon development, large, enduring and long-lived. Thus the Blake-Moulton foundation passed down to myself and brother, and to the cousins who take from that side the heritage of generous stature.

Two generations before me, our branch of the Blake family developed what I believe to have been three able men, my grandfather, John T., and my great uncles, Newell and Ira. My grandfather went to Boston at the age of 20 to learn the boot-maker's trade, and when six years later a death in the family called him home, he immediately enlarged the old tannery building that was family property, and started in business for himself making boots. So well did he succeed that by 1833 we find one of the old Salisbury and Newburyport skippers recording in his diary "that Kensington is the best place for buying either fine or coarse boots."

Old residents of this locality, like Barstow Morril and Joe Nelson, of East Kingston, tell me that in their young days, to wear a pair of boots "of John T. Blake's make" was the acme of fine dressing.

About 40 men worked for my grandfather, some of them in their homes, and some in the old shop, and Kensington became the important Boot-making town above referred to.

And of course in that industrial development shortly before the Civil war, which made Lynn, Haverhill and Newburyport centers from which shoes were sent into surrounding towns to be made up, Kensington very naturally became an important town of shoemakers.

The manufacture of shoes began in this wise in these cities: The "bosses" or manufacturers, secured stock, had it cut, fitted, stitched, and then this material was sent out into the country towns for making. Thus every town about these centers was dotted with little shops about 12 feet square, where two or three neighbors worked shoemaking. Or quite often they worked in their houses.

This form of work was very profitable in early days. Before, and for many years after the war, fine wages were made by these work-men. When the war broke out most of these shoemakers enlisted, for as Whittier so well says of the shoemaker —

"Then yours, at Freedom's trumpet call,
No craftsmen rallied faster."

But at the close of the war, for the most part they returned to take up their work, and Kens-ington continued pre-eminently a shoe-making town.

Shoe freighters, the men who made it their business to make the trips back and forth be-tween the bosses and workmen, were men of considerable importance, and in my early days the most important industrial event was the semi- weekly trip to Haverhill of "Newt" Aus-tin, to take in the made goods, get new stock and pay, for his 100 shoe makers.

In addition to the 100 shoe makers who were supplied by "Newt" Austin, there were some who were supplied by freighters from outside towns, like John L. Chase from Seabrook and Hampton Falls; and there were some who conveyed their own work, so that there must have been considerably over 100 busy shoe makers within the limits of the town.

But the development of machinery, making more and more work to be done in the cities, kept cutting into the individual country workmen; prices kept going down, and finally the first half of the closing decade of the nineteenth century (1890- 1895) saw the hist of the little shops, and all shoe work was moved to the cities. Of course, the springing up of Haverhill, Lynn and Newburyport finished my grandfather's little business, and the old man finished his days at the bench working for those to whom industrial development had given his former position in society.

Among these 125 busy and contented shoemakers who peopled the Kensington of the seventies and eighties was my father, and one of the sounds that came to my ears the second morning I lived on this sphere, must have been the busy tap, tap of his hammer in the adjoining room.

Rap, rap! upon the well worn stone
  How falls the polished hammer;
Rap, rap! the measured sound has grown
  A quick and merry clamor."

Thus Whittier immortalizes in his "Shoe-makers," what must have been my first cradle song. And in the tributes to the sterling qualities of the craft, and the hasty list of the good and great that it has contained which Whittier makes in his poem, I have ever taken pride.

"Let foplings sneer, let fools deride.
  We heed no idle scorner;
Free hands and hearts are still our pride,
  And duty done, our honor."

Thus I was sired and grandsired by the "gentle craft of leather." My first playthings as I crawled upon the floor about my father's bench were the leather chips brushed from his lap. Perhaps it was right there that my socialism, my consciousness of belonging to the working class, began to grow up within me.

These shoemakers were a reliant, intelligent set of men. Working quietly in their homes, or in groups of two or three with abundant opportunity for discussion and thinking, spending their evenings sometimes in visiting a neighbor's shop, listening to the reading of the weekly or daily paper while they worked, they became a very thoughtful and independent set of men. The "gentle craft," it has been called, and Coleridge said in his day that it had produced more distinguished men than any other calling.

Of course, the shoemaking of my early day was very little changed from the old hand craft thru all the ages, and it gave to the world some eminent leaders of men; and better still, it gave us a goodly bulk of an intelligent rank and file. The "gentle craft" had ever been very productive of two honored classes, Quakers and poets; from George Fox down to Whittier, Quakers and poets have come from the shoemaker's bench in large numbers. This would have been a mystery to men seventy years ago, but any Socialist would now see in it but another evidence of economic determination. Modern shoe manufacturers have ofttimes endeavored to silence me in my championship of the shoe workers by saying: "See how much better the shoemaker is to-day; the old hand workman worked twelve to fourteen hours, now the shoemaker works but nine or ten." This is true, but when we recall the old time workman, working leisurely along with his neighbor, or in the bosom of his family; stopping when he chose to smoke his pipe, read his paper, discuss politics, go out and do his chores or hoe his garden; when we contrast this man with the nerve strained feeder of a machine in a great factory, the two or three hours he has gained on the day's length is really no gain at all.

My mother was the ninth and last of Colonel Blake's children, and had taught school at Hampton Falls very nearly up to the time of my birth and resumed the position for a while, as soon after as I was big enough to go along and board with her. I was far from being a robust boy, in fact, the doctor frankly told my parents it would be difficult to raise me, and my mother took a good deal of pains with me.

Thus it was that while other boys were sliding and skating, I was in the house drawing pictures, reading, playing and making things. Other school children came to our fireside to talk over their lessons with my mother or to study with me. My father was also a good deal of a reader, as were my uncles, and so I grew to life feeling with Southey, "That my best days among my books are spent." My parents soon removed to the "Whipple house," on Gove's Hill, and after a few months they moved into one of my grandfather's houses in the little village. This became the Sawyer nest, here my brother and sister were born and here I lived until I left home for good in 1895. Here I passed my uneventful childhood and early days of boyhood. My first religious training was received when I was six. My Uncle Wesley sent me a Christmas present of a suit of clothes, and I was fixed up and sent off to the Congregational Sunday school. Preaching services were morning and afternoon, and I often stayed for the afternoon service. My teachers were at different times: Rosa Akerman, Sidney Chase, and Samuel Batchelder of Hampton Falls; earnest, kindly, faithful teachers, who did their best to instruct me in the fundamental virtues and doctrines of Christianity.

The next spring after I was seven, my mental training was looked after and I was sent off to the common school, the same East school near which I was born. My mother, solicitous for my welfare, hailed Deacon Stephen Brown's team as it returned from church, and secured the chaperonage for me of his son, Stevie, which was faithfully pledged; this same amounted to his securing for me the front seat which no one else wanted, and inducing me to go swimming with him, when under the threat of a ducking, with an additional licking if I told, he secured from me all the pencils that my mother had fitted me out with. I trudged off alone day after day for three years, and the mile and a quarter was a long one, but in 1884 my cousin Esther came to live at the old home and I had company.

My common schooling was largely secured in the summer months, the winters I studied at home. The reason for this was, that in the earlier years the weather was too severe and the trips too long for me, and in later years I could work at home sewing shoes. But my education did not suffer, for cornered in by the table on one side and my father's shoe bench on the other, I was forced to wade thru the Franklin Third Reader and enter upon my first tussles with arithmetic and geography. Undoubtedly the lesson of application to my studies was more thoroly drilled into me than it would have been thru the regular school channels, as my dad had a well appointed rattan handy and was quite severe in using it.

At the age of nine my father removed his

bench from the house to the shop; a brother and sister had been born and the little home of four small rooms was becoming crowded. This left me to the care of my mother, under whom I found the pathway to learning less rugged than under my father, but none the less beneficial, for her former experience as a teacher stood her in good stead, and under her instruction I continued to prosper. It also removed from over me a great deal of strict oversight, and I passed out from being a child to become a boy.

CHAPTER II.

MEMORIES OF BOYHOOD

"Fond memory brings a light
Of other days around me
The smiles and tears
Of boyhood's years."

Tom Moore

"I consider him who writes his own biography the most courteous of men." — GOETHE.

CHAPTER II.

___

MEMORIES OF BOYHOOD

___

URING my boyhood years at Kensington I never rode on a railway train, went to a circus, saw a street parade, visited a pleasure park, traveled more than a dozen miles from home, in fact I had none of those things which the boy of to-day thinks he must have or be miserable, and yet my boyhood was a joyfully contented time. Lacking playmates, both in the family and neighborhood, I developed in early childhood and brought over into boyhood a habit of entertaining myself with original devices of play.

The keen interest that my own children display when I now explain to them the various games that my early ingenuity devised, and a close observation of other children, leads me to believe that I had a knack of entertaining myself that was exceptional. At any rate I do not remember the time when I teased for "something to do." The days were all too short to afford me time to carry out my plans for play, and I never went to bed so tired but that my head was running wild with schemes for another day. With a vivid imagination, I went over and over again with created playthings all that I saw or read about in life. Perhaps my favorite playground was "down in the woods." In this I was undoubtedly helped along by my parents, who, while not offensively religious, insisted that on Sundays I should play down in the woods out of sight. So it was that I climbed the trees, built huts among them or raced about with my brother Wesley and the dog, after my brother was old enough for such. Thus I sowed within myself the seeds of that love for the trees and open life, that now bear fruit in an emotional love of nature so satisfying to me, and by coming back each summer, going bare-foot, living out of doors in the tents, I am able to forget that I am grown up, and I can enjoy life almost as much as I did when a boy. To mark off my boyhood years, both from the childhood that preceded and the youth that followed, is to mark off the period between the time I was 11 years of age to soon after I was 16; these five years I can call my boyhood years.

I do not recall a time when I was too young to want a gun, and I can recollect as tho it were yesterday the first time I ever tired one. It was an old army musket, loaned us boys by Abe Hilliard, and I shot out the top of my hat with a charge of yellow-eyed beans, and went home and hid the ruined headgear in the wood-pile. Accordingly the big event that occurred at the beginning of my boyhood was my coming into possession of a gun, for soon after my birthday my father bought me one and gave it over into my hands. This gun was something that probably I enjoyed more than anything I have owned, or ever shall; it was a little army carbine made over into a shotgun. I named it "Little Forget Me Not," and with it passed some of the happiest hours of my life roaming the woods alert for bird and squirrel. Some of the wise ones among our neighbors were filled with dismay at my having the gun, and predicted that I would shoot myself or someone else, but happily there was never anything ap-proaching a fulfillment of their dire predictions.

Another important fact in this year was my earning the first money I ever earned, which I did by dragging the loafer rake on Newell Healey's farm, and the three one-dollar bills that came to me as pay at the end of the haying season made me feel rich indeed. It was a proud feeling day with the country boys when they got old enough to earn money, and I felt big indeed to think that like my older cousins, the Blake boys, I could earn money, and I proudly spent the sum I received from Newell Healey for store clothes.

Newell was one of the old-fashioned hospitable Yankee farmers, whom the temperance agitators have ever liked to hold up as a horrible example. That is, he put into his cellar a good deal of cider, and kept a good stock of old New England rum always by him. It was hot down there in the hay field, the work was hard. I noticed the men found that work went easier to them by drawing upon that cider jug. And so I, alert to know all the experiences of life, waited till the men went up to the barn with a load of hay, and then drew upon the jug generously. After every load was got into the barn and unloaded, Newell mixed up for himself and the men his toddy (rum, sugar and hot water); this he passed along to me with the rest; it tasted good and I was not averse to taking my turn at it. As might be expected, it did not take much to make me, an eleven-year-old-boy, feel the exhiliarating effects. The feeling was pleasant, and one I came in boyish innocence and ignorance to like to re-produce.

Having learned the winter before, the winter I was 12, I went to work sewing shoes for my father with a stent of eight pairs a day. This summer that I was 12 I worked again for Newell and earned $4, half of which I paid back for a second-hand Waterbury watch. But the great event of this year was not my coming to own a watch, it was rather a great disappointment, one of the greatest that has ever come into my life.

Following the Cleveland election, my Uncle George had been in 1885 appointed local post-master, and in the affluence of that position began to take the Boston Daily *Globe*. This was the first daily paper I had ever seen, and covetously I watched my uncle unwrap it after the mail had been assorted, and long I lingered about that I might catch glimpses of the head-lines, and perhaps get a chance to read a bit. But this uncle was a crusty "old bach," and my chances to see the *Globe* were few, and I labor-iously saved up 50 cents and sent for a month's subscription for myself. Three clays I eagerly watched the mails and then, there came the letter from that for off, mysterious Boston, saying my money had been stolen from the letter. The man who took that 50 cents did me an injury that can never be undone, and my grief was bitter indeed; I guess T have ever nursed that grief, for soon as I got to making $2 a week for sewing shoes I began to take the Boston *Post*, and all my life the one dissipation I have allowed myself is reading the newspapers.

This fall my fathers' cousin George turned up at our house. George was a carriage painter; he had been all over the country, hoboed it, worked it, beat it, and in turn accepted its hard knocks. George opened up a paintshop in an unused part of the old shop, and as we were near the carriage making town of Amesbury, Mass., soon had a lot of business, and things boomed more than ever in the little village. This winter I increased my stent of work to fifteen pairs a day, did not go to school at all and was much with the men, and as times were much rougher in those days than now, and as many of these shoemakers were men who had worked away in the cities, while others were soldiers returned from the war, it must be confessed that they were not overnice about the character of their amusements, nor fussy about what their influence on young life might be.

I learned to smoke and chew, to play cards, read the Beadle's "Dimes and Half-Dimes," family story papers and Police Gazettes, and generally take part in that which made up the amusements of the men about me. The next year I was fourteen, and it was about the same as the year before, save that my stent of work moved up to eighteen pairs of shoes per day.

The North road boys began in the early eighties to go to Exeter to see the Academy boys play baseball with their rivals from Phillips Andover; in this way baseball was introduced into Kensington, and soon displaced the games of "three-old-cat," rolling truck, etc. Thru my touch with the North road boys, and also from my own attendance upon the games at Exeter, I learned the game and introduced it into the East school. We had then about 30 pupils at the school, so there were abundant to play, and it brightened up my school life and made it much more attractive to me. But not only in play was the school attractive to me, I entered into its serions business with a real joy.

It was run on the old ungraded plan, the only plan where ability and earnestness can really count, and so I could make up readily for what I lost by winter absence. And under that plan the personality of the teacher, and her interest in the pupil went further than in a graded school, and so I can record my eternal indebtedness to my principal teachers, Lizzie Titcomb, Sadie Chase, Rosa Akerman and Anna Lamprey.

Centers of social life in many New England towns in the years following the war were the "local divisions" of the "Sons of Temperance." Ours was named the "Hoosac Division," and as I was now old enough to join, my chum, Pat Hilliard, and I joined. Pat and I behaved so badly that he was suspended and I was expelled. Pat's father kept the local store, was a leading Republican and worth some few thousands of dollars; my father was a shoemaker; this marked the difference in our treatment by the "division."

Thus, even in the old town life of New England, which was ideally so democratic, with the village squire and cobbler thoro equals, there were social distinctions, drawn on econo-

mic inequalities; and social classes will ever
exist 80 long as economic inequalities continue.
Expulsion from the division did not disturb
me, but it did Pat, and more especially his
father, who now put over him a more strict
oversight. So it happened that on January 5,
1889, Pat came into the shop where I was
helping my father, and waiting till my father
had gone to dinner, proposed that we "run off."

I had no grievance, but answered that I
would start as soon as I got dinner. Accordingly, as soon as we got dinner, I made some
excuse to my father, and Pat and I started.
We traveled thru several towns and reached
Newburyport that night. Pat and I huddled
away in a freight car bound for St. Louis, but
the vigilant yard watchman routed us out and
drove us away. It was a cold night, and Pat
and I had no recourse but to join the line of
hoboes to the station house. Here we spent
the night with some twenty-five professional
tramps, out-of-works and drunks in the cells.
It was the first night I had ever slept away from
my home, and I got an impressive lesson of the
real kindness that exists among the brotherhood
of unfortunates. We shared with the rest in
the work of the morning, sweeping, cleaning

spittoons, etc., but when it came to going out with the rest as we had planned the night before, the vigilant cops spotted us for a couple of runaways, and detained us. Three days, or until I had celebrated my fifteenth birthday (January 8, 1889), we were held up, and then no communication reaching the police we were allowed to venture forth. "Where now," I asked Pat. "Home," was the monosyllable reply, and home it was. A bracing walk of twelve miles across country on top of the scanty rations at the police station brought to us two boys an awful appetite, and we held up at a little shoeshop in front of a farmhouse, where I sewed shoes for some apples. Later, a Kensington boy that I knew took us to a French woodchopper's hut and fried us some potatoes and we reached home at nightfall to ease our distracted folks. The rehearsal of our exploits made us considerable of heroes with our boy friends.

I had been the creator and keeper of a hut in the woods called "The Hunter's Home." It was a rendezvous where we boys retired to smoke on the sly, read dime novels, play cards, eat stolen watermelons, fruit, etc., and make game chowders when we shot anything. I now determined on something larger, and in view of the free rein my folks gave me lest I run away again, I was able to carry out my plans. So it was that we boys united in stealing enuf boards of various descriptions to make a larger shanty, which we called the Devil's Den. Here we had a better retreat, one that was heated, and where evening and Sunday gatherings for smoking, reading and card playing at a cent ante and 50 cent limit, could be indulged in to our heart's content. I now began to sell the weekly illustrated paper, the Utica Globe, and a little later the Manchester Saturday Telegram. Thus I spent Saturday afternoons and evenings visiting the little shoeshops, saw mills, farmers' homes. This paper selling was a thing of big importance to me, it afforded me capital for Sunday poker playing, or often to match a paper against a nickle in a game of pitch or "High-lo-Jack;" but on the other hand it gave me my first intellectual interest in the great big outside world. T began to make scrap books, get interested in what was going on.

I had reached the limit of the Kensington common schools, and in September I began at the high school in Exeter. I went the fall and winter terms, but the spring term had hardly begun when, owing partly to the long dreary walk of eight miles a day, and the fact that my interest was in anything but books, and that like the older boys I wanted to be earning my own money, I gave up school and went to work in the shop. My father was a careful workman, had taught me well and I was a good "seamer." Thus ended my boyhood.

CHAPTER III

THE DAYS OF MY YOUTH

"The days of my youth have gone by."

Old Song.

"Remember not the sins of my youth."

David.

"When in the slippery paths of youth
  My wayward steps they ran,
Thine arm unseen conveyed me safe
  And led me up to man."

Old Hymn.

"It is the object of autobiography to relate the facts of one's life, not to apologize for them," — BEN FRANKLIN.

CHAPTER III

———

THE DAYS OF MY YOUTH

———

THERE can never again be possible on this planet another youth like, mine, because the industrial conditions of life can never again be what they were in the shoemaking region of New England in the thirty years following the civil war. During this period the development of machinery was in just that stage to develop a new generation, a new type of human life, with its joys and sorrows. A sort of semi-industrial semi-agricultural type.

As I have before remarked, the times were rough: two thirds of the shoemakers in our town had spent three or four years in the army during the war, and many others had drifted about the country. This class of men were of course not much concerned that we of the younger generation should grow up with thoughtful and serious habits.

It must not be supposed, however, that there

were not many in the older generation who did not look askance at the fast habits of the boys of my day.

It was something quite new to many of the old quiet hand workmen, aud the slower moving farmers.

But in Haverhill, twenty miles away, and in Lynn, forty miles away, a new type was growing up. Machinery was coming, better wages were there, young men were going there to work. Hundreds of young unmarried men and women, thus thrown together removed from the old restraining influence of their country homes, were developing forms of enjoyment that were quite shocking to their parents at home. Older boys returning to the country towns told of the big times off in Haverhill and Lynn, and gave to us younger ones quite different ideals from what we would have contented ourselves with but for them.

Up the river were Lawrence, Lowell, Manchester and Nashua; large textile cities full of Irish- Americans and French-Canadians

There were thousands of poorly paid but handsome young women in these cities. The Catholic church had taught, like Roosevelt, that big families were divinely ordered, thus lads and misses swarmed to the mills. It did not take long for the unscrupulous to link together sex and liquor for profit. And so out of the girls who came down to Haverhill to make their fortune and missed it, and from the poorly paid girls in the mill cities, the roadhouses were equipped. The era of "sporting life" that thrived for about twenty years in the industrial regions was that into which the stream of life threw me. How could I but be a part of it?

I was sixteen when I went into the shop to do a man's work. Of course doing a man's work gave me the right to a man's habits, amusments and vices; why not? So I smoked, chewed my ten cent piece of tobacco daily, played cards and drank with the rest. Summers I lounged about, riding the bicycle and playing baseball. There was, however, on my part a growing dissatisfaction with the life, and a growing of a more serious side within me.

On my seventeenth birthday I made some serious resolutions, and on my eighteenth had developed quite a thorough-going religious feeling, and I made some resolutions about drinking, and on February 29 stopped it altogether.

Thus two and a half years went quickly by.

THE DAYS OF MY YOUTH

In September, 1892, I went to work for a while in an Exeter restaurant. I had worked but ten days when there came to me a breakdown in health. I went to my room one night after an evening spent in playing pool. It was a free pool table in a saloon, and as I was on the "water wagon," I took cigars, which meant that I consumed a more than ordinary amount of the cheap black stogies that the New Hampshire bar-room, under the temperance regime of the grand old party of moral reform, used to serve up. Anyway, a severe attack of heart affection came upon me, and the next day I went home to Kensington. "The days of my youth had gone by," for three years I was to hang about the town trying to get back my health, and to develop my hold on the more serious things of life that should ultimately lead me out to where I am today. This awaits telling in the next chapter.

In telling the story of my childhood and youth in these two chapters, I believe I am more than giving a little sketch of my personal life. I believe I am drawing a little picture that has permanent value. I am lifting the curtain a little, to show to men what life meant to the working people in one branch of the great industrial revolution of the nineteenth century. Very early men saw that they must have some protection for their feet, and human ingenuity was taxed to provide it. This developed the craft of shoemaking. Pictures from ancient Egypt show that up to less than forty years ago this craft had changed very little. The old craftsmen, who all over the New England states, but especially in Massachusetts and New Hampshire, were in 1875 working away with pegs, awl, hammer and lapstone, were not very far ahead of the old Egyptians 5,000 years before them. Then came machinery as applied to shoemaking, and in less than thirty years the old shoemaker was a thing of the past. With his little 10 x 12-foot shop, his waxed ends and lapstone, he disappeared forever. Shoe manufacture advanced at a leap to be one of our greatest industries. McKay shoes displaced the coarse boots that my grandfather made, and welts displaced his fine boots.

A quarter of a million toilers today in the factories of America make 250,000,000 pairs of shoes a year. And all this great industry is capitalistically organized into an ironclad monopoly to which the millions of men and women wearing shoes pay tribute and which is the

master of the lives and destinies of these 250,
000 workmen. There is no chapter in modern
industrial and commercial development more
interesting and more characteristic than that
of shoemaking. This sudden jump, all in a
generation, meant that some men should find
themselves suddenly elevated from the humble
position of a boss, expecting little above his
workmen, to become magnates with thousands
and even millions of dollars.

It is the same in all manufacture. And
by shrewdly manipulating public thought
these manufacturers, this new dominant economic class, has been able to make people think
that they are in a way superior to the men who
still run the machines and do the work.

Of course this has not been so hard to do as
one might think, for men always think in the
terms of their economic experiences, and the
manufacturer has but to insist that the economic conditions of the last generation still prevail,
and the deed is done. For it is true that the
first "bosses" did most always get their start
by thrift and extra denial, but what was true
of the last generation is not true of this.

For instance, I recall a well known boss in
Haverhill by the name of Osgood; he was origin-

ally a cutter, and by saving his money he bought some stock for a case of shoes, worked nights and cut them, sent them to a contract shop and had them fitted and stitched, sent them out to Kensington to be made, and then sent them to a commission house in Boston where they were sold, and he made $30 on the proceeding. He repeated this operation, soon he left working for another and worked all the time for himself, then he regularly employed others, and in time became a prosperous manufacturer and worth perhaps $25,000.

But such an experience is no longer possible, for today a man must own or control a great factory and complicated machinery, in order to manufacture shoes.

No working man can by working nights and saving, ever save enuf to buy a factory and mechanical system worth hundreds of thousands of dollars. Thus today the manufacturer is no longer a man of greater thrift, energy or ability; he is simply the man, who by hook or by crook, (generally by inheritance) possesses money enuf to enable him to own a factory.

But this man cunningly plays upon the experiences of the past generation—he knows men are slow to think, stupid to learn of out.

grown conditions, and so by controlling the preachers, teachers, editors, politicians, the employing capitalist˙ class is able to make this bluff go. These men are not men of superior ability, they are men for the most part who were in the position whereby industrial evolution thrust their success upon them, and they have been cunning enuf to maintain their position.

To illustrate, I think now of a manufacturer by name of Spalding most of whose shoes were made in Kensington. Jimmie Austin of our town, with members of his family, made many shoes for Spalding, When the new sewing machines came out, Jimmie was one of the first in our locality to get oue.

When Spalding first learned of this he cussed and swore, and said, "damned if I will ever have a machine—sewed shoe in my shop." He took his work away from Jimmie and kept his position for a few years till the machines got in everywhere and then he was forced to give them a trial. Within five years he had incorporated machinery in his factory, and he is now a highly successful captain of the shoe industry, basking during his declining years, in the praises of press and pulpit, of being one of

those men of "exceptional fore-sight and capacity." And yet it was not fore-sight or ability, he simply had his economic success thrust
upon him, and he has *bought* all the rest.

Thus it is with all lines of industry, with all
these great "manufacturers." These men became this not because of greater ability, but
because they were in a position to seize the
control and ownership of this new thing, this
machinery. There was more difference in
the ability between my grandfather and his
workmen than between W. L. Douglas or
George E. Keith and his, but it did not profit
my grandfather anything in money. Of course
this great jump also meant a big wrench to the
ideas, life and morals of the people, the humble shoemakers who were caught in that generation.

I was one of these, and I believe my humble
sketch has value as giving a little insight into
what it meant to us, the people, who were
born to the lapstone, but were shifted to the
machine.

CHAPTER IV

MY START IN LIFE

"I came that you might have a life more abund-
ant."   *Jesus of Nazareth,*

"Any man interested in himself is interesting to other men," — WENDELL PHILIPS.

CHAPTER IV

———

PREPARATION FOR THE SERIOUS SIDE OF LIFE

———

P to the breakdown in my health when I was eighteen years of age, my chief ambition had been to push on and secure a standing in the sporting world. Some little experience with running, boxing, ball playing had stirred within me hopes of personal achievement along some of these lines, and I looked ahead to my height of ambition as a proprietor of a sporting hotel. This was all at one blow put aside. The political contest of 1892 was coming on. My family were all Democrats and excited at Cleveland's prospects, and I set myself diligently at work reading all the political speeches and discussing the outlook, at the sessions for such, held daily in one of the two local cross-roads stores.

A local celebration of Columbus' Day was to be held on October 12 at the town hall, and I

wrote some verses for my sister Elizabeth to
speak, which were published by the county
paper.

This much pleased me, and I followed it with
political letters, correspondence, etc. Thus it
happened that my ambitions underwent a rapid
change. My grandfather had been for many
years the big man in our little town—colonel
of the training company, justice of peace,
moderator, representative of legislature for six
terms, etc. I now began to aspire to follow
in his steps. Accordingly after Cleveland's
election I applied to the local Democratic com-
mittee to be made postmaster. The matter hung
along for a while, but finally was passed by.

This led the way for my advent into cross-
road politics. In the campaign of 92 I had
come under the magic spell of a really great
man, Governor Altgeld of Illinois. I quickly
detected in his speeches a different ring from
that of the Cleveland camp. An old school-
mate was now an edge trimmer in Lynn, an en-
thusiast in the ranks of the Knights of Labor
and a Populist, and he was sending me labor
and Populist literature. The little group of
Populists at Washington, of whom Jerry Simp-
son was the most interesting figure, expressed

about what I felt, and so I became a Populist, I worked hard on my schemes, and by the Spring election in 1894 I had gathered together a People's party which united with the Republicans, and we overthrew the Democrats who had ruled the town for over thirty years.

Then came the Debs-Pullman strike in July. I espoused the cause of Debs, and championed the workers' side in many a fierce discussion at the stores, and passed along to take such radical positions as to destroy my political hold upon the conservative farmers, and thus to defeat my hopes of political success. To understand what this sacrifice of political aspiration meant to me, what it cost me to follow my sympathies for the working class, my conscience and my intelligence, one must know a little more of my position at the time.

There is probably no state in the union that has more politics than New Hampshire, and Rockingham county (my county) leads New Hampshire. At that time the Democratic party in the state was Frank Jones, the Portsmouth brewing capitalist, and Boston and Maine railroad director. The Republican party was the rest of the Boston and Maine officials. Of course, there was a big bulk of rank and file who went thru various motions, voted, held offices and the like, but these motions were intelligible only to these aforesaid parties. I don't know that Jones and the Boston and Maine began bribery in the state, but they developed it to a fine art. Most any election in the smaller towns of New Hampshire, and especially Rockhingham county, could give cards and spades to the Ohio exposures and beat them easily.

In New Hampshire we have one of the largest legislative bodies in the world, nearly 400 members. Every little town sends its representative, and seldom does a man get the office without spending $300 or $400, and the defeated candidate spends about as much. The Democratic town committees in Rockingham county went to Jones before each election, got orders and the sinews of war, $300, $400, or $500, as the case demanded. The republican committees drew upon the Boston and Maine for theirs.

Votes in my little town seldom went for less than $ 15, and ranged up to $30, or even $35.

Since I have left it the voting list has fallen to less than 100, but it still takes about $400 to elect a representative. The Hon. Frank Jones was our big man in the county.

It must be remembered that the state was then under the Prohibition law, and manned by Republican officials, the party of grand moral ideals. This law was really the permission of free rum . Exeter and Portsmouth, shire towns in the county, had one bar-room for about every ninety people, and the little towns that run alongside the Massachusetts line near Haverhill, were sown down with roadhouses. The only restriction laid upon these places was that they stand arrest once a year and contribute a fine of $ 100 and costs toward running the county expenses, and that they handle Jones' beer. Jones was a contributor to charitable affairs, to churches and the like, and so far as I know, newspapers and ministers never raised their voices against him.

About the first practical political work I ever did was to go the rounds of some of these resorts, just before election, with Jones' sheriff, Eddie Coffin, and give out the list of Jones' candidates and remind them that a good vote was wanted. I was getting onto the inside of this, and with my ability had good reason to suppose that I might rapidly rise, and at that time had, of course, no thought of anything else in mind, so it was a soul-struggle for me to go over with Debs and the radical Populists, and denounce political conditions under Democratic and Republican rule.

But I have never regretted it; a county, or even a state office in such a stink-pot is, after all, nothing very great, and New Hampshire today is not very far ahead of New Hampshire then, tho I admit it is somewhat. I said there was no restriction on liquor selling in Rockingham county, save that Jones' beer be handled and the annual fine be paid; there was one thing more in Exeter. Exeter is the home of the Phillips Academy, the preparatory school for Harvard College. Up to this institution come the youth of New England's wealthy and aristocratic families. Of course it would not do to put open temptation under the noses of these youths, so Exeter rigidly enforced the law that liquor should not be sold to these boys.

I recall going into a place one night, a stripling of sixteen, and calling for a glass of ale. The bartender shook his head. I expostulated, but in vain, and was just turning away when I laid one of my hands upon the bar rail. Instantly his keen eyes saw the shoe blacking upon my fingers, he reached for the tank lever and drew my ale. My hands had shown that

I was just a workingman's boy, not an upper class youths as he at first thought; and, of course, Exeter did not mind how much booze was sold to the boys of the working class.

Interesting, amusing and informing reminiscences come before me as I am writing, but I forego to put them down, for they are but corroborative evidence of what is now so plain to all who will see, viz., that the corruption of politics then was—as the corruption of politics is now—the alert hand of business seizing hold of political power. Doing this in the interest of profit, and using the only thing it knows as power—money. Such was capitalism developing; such is capitalism fullgrown; such will be capitalism forever. Clean politics can never come till private profit goes. In a spasmodic wave of virtue the two candidates in the near town of Kingston one year pledged themselves to spend no money. Uncle John, a man who always sold his vote (and well to do farmers do this thing year after year), waited about the polls two hours and no one offered him a cent, and so he trudged off toward home. Meeting a fellow townsman, who asked him why he had not voted. Uncle John told of his waiting, and receiving no offers, and grunting out, "It's no use the country's gone to hell, anyway," he continued off home. We smile at the old man and his ideas of the duties of citizenship, but the average understanding or attempt at reform on the part of old party reformers is but little more intelligent.

When I start to recall the amusing incidents illustrating political corruption under capitalist politics, I hardly know where to stop.

I remember my father going one election day with his team to get a man whom the republicans had bribed to stay away. He got the man and was returning with him, when he met a man by the name of Evans. Evans was a democrat, and the way he was legging it away from the town-hall told my father what was up. Upon inquiry my father found that Evans had received $25 from the republicans if he would stay away from the election. Evans had the money in his pocket all safe, and so he accepted $20. from my father to come back to election and vote democratic. There was jubilation among the democrats when my Father drove up with Evans and told the instance, but it was short lived, for the republicans got hold of Evans again before the democrats could get him to cast a ballot, and by giving him another $15, secured from him a vote for the "grand old party of moral ideals".

A more amusing incident occured one election when we had the old fashioned sheet ballot, all candidates printed on one slip. The election was running close, and there was a man in town of whom the republicans were afraid, even if he took their money, so they decided to give him $10 to go to Exeter to stay over election day.

The election day was well along before the democrats got alive to the trick, and then they dispatched a team to Exeter for this man. The desired man was found at Levi Towle's tavern, and he had made such good use of his money that he was drunk as a lord.

In 25 minutes a foam covered democratic horse halted before the door of Kensington Town-Hall, and the man steadied toward the ballot box, with a democratic ballot in his hand, and $ 15 democratic money in his pocket. The chagrined republicans sent a man to him who steadied the other side and thrust a G. O. P ballot into the other hand . Just as the trio reached the ballot-box, the town's one prohibitionist, a deaf mute, thrust into the man's hand a prohibition ballot, and the drunken fellow seized upon the way out of the dilemma, and before he could be prevented cast the temperance ticket. He beat both sides and voted the prohibition ticket, tho drunk at the time.

After the Australian ballot law was passed, various devices were put forth to defeat its aim, and oft-times it was disregarded by mutual consent, the bribers taking their position each side of the entrance and trusting to out bid one another in the purchase of votes.

Somewhere between my seventeenth and eighteenth birthdays 1 developed an interest in religion. At first this seems to have been just a feeling that came to me, and then in seeking expression I first fell under the spell of the Catholic church. I was at just at that impressionable age where the grandeur of her service, ritual and imagery could not but exert a large influence over me. For about a year after my break-up in health this same feeling for the Catholic church continued. But I was mentally distressed by my sickness, and read the Bible and such tracts and books as I could find, with the result that I finally came to the conviction that Universalists and Unitarians came nearest to expressing my feeling in matters religious. On April 19, 1894, I attended a serenade at

Sherm Shaw's, a farmer in the northern part of our town, and was called upon to make the presentation speech of some little token we were leaving. Without any thought as to the matter I arose, my heart thumped, my face flushed, the stillness was simply awful; forty pairs of eyes were upon me and they seemed a million. I made a few scattered remarks, pulled my hair for an idea in vain, and sat down chagrined, but vowing in my heart to overcome that feeling at any cost.

It was at about this time that a new minister came to town, David Fraser, a young man and interested in the younger people. He got up a Christian Endeavor Society; I joined, tho it must be admitted that a good part of my purpose was to have a chance to practice talking. I proposed a debating society and we put it thru. Thus I developed some ability as a speaker, and very naturally it came about that my friend, the minister, suggested that I study for the ministry. I had just attended the Chritian Endeavor convention in Boston, was quite full of religious enthusiasm; the idea seemed good, there was nothing else insight, and I determined to try it.

For many years the theological seminaries had what they called "an English course"—a course of study adapted to just such men as my-self. But professional pride among the min-isters, made the doctors of divinity object to a man coming into the ministry with a few years' study, and standing equal with them, after they had put in the full college and academic training. Especially did they become hot when some of these "short course" men, like Smith Baker et al, went far ahead of them in profes-sional popularity; so it was that these English courses were cut out. Then it was that a pro-phet arose, the Rev. Joseph Bixby, of Revere, a suburb of Boston. He organized an English course seminary at Revere, and called it "Lay College." His idea was to have an institution of, for and by the people.

It was this institution that the Rev. Eraser came from, and to it I turned my steps on Oc-tober 7, 1895. I was now twenty-one years of age. For the three years past I had read miles of newspapers and magazines, using Exeter and Amesbury reading rooms and friendly news-dealers to supply me. But extended study of books was a new thing. 1 soon found, however, I was going to make a go of it, so I came home, sold out my game roosters, joined the church and settled down to become a minister.

While at Revere the '96 campaign came along. I had much faith and hope in the Bryan move-ment, wrote some and spoke some for "free silver" and voted for Bryan and Watson.

After the defeat of the cause of silver and Bryan and the beginning of the end for Populism, I began to go to Socialist meetings somewhat in Boston and Lynn. Herbert Casson was at this time running a labor church out at Lynn, in an old abolition church building on Oxford street. He was a pronounced and radical Socialist at the time, and had for a time quite an enthusiastic following among the Socialists, trades unionists and radicals. I went out to this church a good deal. But Casson's church finally broke up. The Socialist movement in Boston and Lynn was a strongly proletarian Socialist-Labor movement, and I found no very hearty welcome, being now out of the wage-working class, so I began to fall away from the political things and to work harder and closer on the books. Thus it came to pass that by my graduation, in 1898, I had turned mv back entirely upon my earliest ambition to enter politics thru the ministry, and was ready to give several years to the straight-out ministerial round of work.

The teachings at Revere were of the strict old-fashioned type, emphasizing the old doctrines and conceptions. The ascetic, ecstatic side of religious experience was made much of.

I had imbibed all this. Again I had worked thru the three years in the face of many hardships as to health, struggling on when at times it seemed I must let it all go. So it was that I turned my step from the school to the ministry with a soul full of religious fervor and a consecration of spirit beyond the average.

If ever any man entered upon the work of a Gospel minister with high ideal, with devotion to duty, with the expectation of doing great things, it was myself. Hot with this religious enthusiasm, having accepted with all sincerity the work of my calling, it remained for me to encounter the awful jolt of running up against modern life in capitalist society. I was to find that service in any successful church was a mere commercial thing, and that genuine loyalty to Jesus and His gospel was largely lost in the grab for dollars. That in the church where I expected to find men and women eager to join hands with me in helping humanity there were few who cared for poor humanity. That among those to whom I looked for the most unselfish service, was the spirit of the age so strong that altruism was largely stamped out. So severe a jolt was this that it was to take a long time for me to be conquered, and it must be told in the next chapter of my story.

52

CHAPTER V

BEFORE I HIT THE TRAIL

"God be thanked — whatever comes,
I have lived and toiled with men."
"The Galley Slave."

"Memoirs or Journals written not because of historical or political significance, hut because they are to the writer the natural expression of what life meant to him, in the moment of living, have a value entirely apart from literary quality."
MYRTLE LOCKETT AVERY.

CHAPTER V

———

BEFORE I HIT THE TRAIL

———

AM on my fourteenth year as a minister, and these years fall naturally into three divisions, which I shall tell about in three chapters, entitled, "Before I hit the Trail." "Finding My Way" and "The Open Road." I began to look about for a church during my last year at the Revere school, and found out that a "short course" man could receive no assistance from our denominational organizations, and that from many of the clergy he could get a pretty warm opposition. But I finally secured a hearing at Brockton, in the South Congregational church, whose pastor, William Thomas Beale, was every inch a man, and declared he only wanted a man who was capable and did not care where his diploma was signed, and so I was taken on as his associate and the acting pastor at Hope Chapel. I began my work at

Brockton in February, 1898, going out Friday nights and returning Monday mornings, till school closed in May, when I moved there, boarding the home of a shoe-laster, Henry Lake. With the state of my health and my temperament a home of my own was a necessity, to say nothing about my sentiments for a young lady back in my native town, and so on June 29 I was married to Mary L. Palmer of Kensington. We had a little wedding at the home of her parents with about 50 friends present, spent a few days at Hampton Beach, and then returned to Brockton, having the fine courage but poor judgment, to start housekeeping on $90 in ready money, a few debts and a $500 salary.

DeWitt Talmadge is authority for the statement that the first pastorate of a preacher is his hardest, and it certainly is.

This was especially so in my 'case, with a ceaseless round of pastoral calls, two sermons to be ground out each week, few books to help, meager training, and bound with that conscientiousness which is quite often a minister's till the new wears off, I worked hard. Then again I had not learned to say "no" to the numerous gospel missions, temperance societies and the like that sponge a whole lot on a preacher in a city. My service was in the afternoon and evening and left me free to go to the aid of any other preacher who wanted to be off on a Sunday; I was easy picking for such ministers, and I performed many a service for them; they were always profuse in thanks, tho I don't recall a single instance where one of them ever paid me, tho some of them got good money.

The Campello Congregational church, which hired me is one of the finest plants in New England. Its head at that time (and now) was George E. Keith the millionaire shoe manufacturer, tho there were other manufacturers and business men associated with him. Of these men I have no words save to record their kindness, patience with me, and readiness to help in church work, as they understood it. In fact I think these men invariably are kind to their pastors; they give them shoes, clothing, knock down prices in trade, etc. They recognize that the preacher is many times a poor devil struggling along on wholly inadequate pay, and donations and the like are much better than increased salaries. Larger salaries would mean more independent preachers, while donations leave him under obligations to the giver, he cannot very well find fault with the way they run business if he is at the same time a recipient of their bounty. Thus gifts and kindness to pastors are a sort of bribe, tho such is the blindness caused by the deep-seated errors of capitalism, that with both bribed and bribers it is largely unconscious. And the type of teaching in the churches is a good bit to blame. I recall a conversation with a young shoe manufacturer in which he unburdened his soul to me, and declared his soul struggles. He was an athletic young fellow, not long out of college, a fine, conscientious fellow, and he confided to me that it was an awful cross for him in the fall of the year not to look at the Sunday newspapers that contained the accounts of the Saturday football games in which he was much interested.

This young fellow took the church seriously, was determined to follow its teachings, he did so, and these teachings led him to find in Sunday newspapers, theatre going and card playing, the great sins of the day. He abstained from these and thought he was doing God's will; he had no conception of "doing justly, loving mercy and walking humbly with God," which the Hebrew Prophet told us 2700 years ago was true religion rather than ceremonies and penances.

In the light of my present knowledge my mental position at that time was one in which the ridiculous and pathetic were mingled. I could not keep away from trying to argue some answer to the criticisms that the social prophets were beginning to make with the church, but every time I talked over the matter with my serious minded friends, they always took the position that "a man's business does not have anything to do with his religion," and as it was perfectly obvious that business could not succeed on any religious basis, this seemed to me the only answer.

And yet I was not easy—it seemed to me that somehow business ought not to be contrary to religion, especially when most of the successful business men were so active religious leaders—but I was not yet ready to follow Jesus and Tolstoy, and so I tramped about lost in intelectual and moral fog.

I guess I had a pretty good start-off there in Brockton to make for myself a successful ministerial career, but somehow it wasn't in me to follow the narrow limits of the conventional ministerial life. The Philippine war came on, and I took it upon myself to set forth the truth about that, viz—that commercial exploitation, yellow journalism and jingoism was all that was back of it, that to send young men over there to kill, plunder and burn the Filipinos for doing what we did in 1775 was the crime of the ages. Of course, this brought the G. A. R. to their feet in indignant protest, and under the lead of an ex-Methodist minister they plastered me with resolutions, lamenting my existence on the planet, and when my chapel caught fire on the Fourth of July they tried to make it appear that it was indignant and hot-headed citizens trying to burn me out; but it later appeared to be the work of a cracked fire-bug.

Then came the Boer war, and I joined with the Irish in getting Maud Gonne and other speakers to the city and we showed up Great Britain in her true colors. Then there was the lasters' strike. The Lasters' Union in Brockton was then a fighting organization, before Tobin's uuion was thought of. A shoe manufacturer once said to me, speaking of Tobin's union, "if we had worked for years we could not have gotten up a scheme so good for the manufact-urer as this union of Tobin's." Of course not, it stands for arbitration, and that, before the board of politicians appointed by the manufacturer's governor, the shoe-worker finds the cards stacked in the game. But I championed the lasters' strike.

Then it was during these months that Debs and Berger and the rest met at Chicago to organize the Socialist party. Margaret Haile came to Brockton to report on the meeting. To listen to her report there were I think eight present besides myself and wife, mostly these eight were, like myself ex-Populists. Then came one of the wonderful things; it was voted to organize a local, a ticket was put into the field, and the first year got 600 votes. Another year and Coulter, Socialist mayor, was elected by a majority over both old parties. Tho I did not join the local, I invited them to my church to hear me preach. I advocated the election of the Socialist ticket and did what I could to bring that result to pass. Coulter called upon me to be the chaplain at his inauguration as second Socialist mayor to be elected in the United States. Chase of Haverhill having been elected as the first. Many of the comrades urged that I join the party and run as alderman in my ward, and later as representative. Had I done this, election would have followed in both cases without doubt, but I had not yet come to see that activity in public matters was impossible for a minister, tho my dabbling in labor and political matters was a subject upon which my friends in the church earnestly protested against and warned me fully of what the effects would be upon my chance of professional success.

It was at Brockton that my first child was born (Ruth, now 12 and an ardent Socialist), and I knew that Shakespeare must have been a father to feel the words he put into Henry's mouth —

"Before this happy child, never did I get any
    thing:
This oracle of comfort hath so pleased me,
That when I am in heaven, I shall desire
To see what this child does, and praise my
    maker."

But I wanted to study further, and so after two and one half years at Brockton I secured a location at Hanson, ten miles away, and in August, 1900, moved there. Hanson I found to be the typical Pilgrim district town, with its little white church on the hill, its cosy parsonage, and its warm-hearted people thoroly indifferent to all things religious. I began at once to study in Boston University and went two years, the most important courses being those under the late Professor Bowne and President Warren. Bowne was one of the acutest speculative thinkers this country has produced, but he was a thoro-going heartless aristocrat, and commended the policy of giving the ignorant laborers a leather suit and six cents a day and setting them at work. He one morning took the entire session to justify big fortunes and salaries as the reward of ability, and laid especial stress upon the various high-salaried presidents of the life insurance companies. But within a few months the exposures came and we found the same men the embodiments of inefficiency and corruption. The Revere school had undergone a reorganization, and was now called the Boston Evangelical Institute, and I was elected one of the instructors, which work I carried on for three years, then there came a break, and I received of my salary but little more than enuf to pay my expenses.

While at Hanson I also organized the Anti-Profanity League, the first endeavor along those lines to be made in the Protestant Church at least, and it sedured a large following of over 20,000 members in this country and other lands, and the indorsement of King Edward, Roosevelt, Justice Harlan, Talmadge and a lot of the big preachers. Thus during my four and a third years at Hanson I did my share of regular religious work, and did it with little other pay than my $650 a year and house rent.

Hanson was in MacCartney's district, and I did what little I could to keep him on Beacon Hill. MacCartney was the Unitarian minister who left his church at Rockland to become the Socialist representative. When he died some of the Comrades approached me about joining the party and running for the place, but I was not yet willing to believe that a Socialist could not succeed as a minister.

While I voted the Socialist ticket most of the time, yet I did not confine myself to it. One of my deacons was a very ardent Prohibitionist, and I went in 1900 to his county convention with him, and allowed my name to go on their ticket for a county office, and I was flattered by the vote of 1800 I got as against 150 for the ticket's head. And when the 1904 campaign approached I was one of those who were drawn into the Hearst movement. Hearst was trying to secure the presidential nomination. I went to Boston as state delegate for Hearst, and remained affiliated with his party till I united with the Socialist party four years later.

The Psalmist says something about the godly man being blessed with his quiver full of children. Anyway three more came into my quiver while at Hanson, a girl and two boys, Rachel, Roland Darrow and Robert.

November 13, 1904, I preached my farewell sermon at Hanson ; the next day I began dismantling my cozy home, and a week later began my work at the Ward Hill church in Haverhill.

I had now got the hang of things in the ministry pretty well. I had the friendship of the Rev. Drs. Smith Baker, Plumb and Withrow, the last great figures of the old guard in New England Congregationalism; they had befriended me, taken part in my ordination and installation and so on. I brought forth things "new and old" in a sermonic way for the people, the congregation built up and the work moved on finely at the Ward Hill church.

I still adhered to the older theological conceptions, and from considerable reading in history, literature and current events, I was able to put these things before the people in a very pleasing way to them.

Unsolicited approaches from larger pulpits began to creep in to me. Tho I mixed into political and public matters too much to suit some, and my radical tendencies were known, yet still I was essentially safe, and anyhow progressive ideas were filtering thru, and there was a chance for me ahead. We were now within 20 miles of the boyhood home, practically on the old stamping grounds, and thus two and one half years slipped by, and then—then came the awakening. I stumbled onto the path, I hit the trail, I found the way—but I must leave the telling of that for my next chapter.

CHAPTER VI

FINDING MY WAY

"Blessed is he who finds his work."

Carlyle's Beatitude.

*"It is the duty of all upright and credible men, to faith-
fully record the principle events in their lives."*

Benvenuto Cellini.

CHAPTER VI

———

FINDING MY WAY

———

HE year 1906 passed rapidly on; my fifth child, a little girl, Rosalind Blake, was born on June 17. This meant a busy summer and little vacation, and an added scrutinizing of expenses to get by on my $900 salary, but we did it, the exact figure being $804.

I was still affiliated with the Hearst movement and supported John B. Moran for governor. Moran was really a strong character, fearless and honest. The local Democracy ran me for alderman, and my support was flattering to me, being a vote of 1,600, the top of the list and twice that of the head of the ticket. Thus we come up to December, that time when a bomb was dropped into my mental life, and which launched me away on a voyage of fifteen months' reading and thinking, that was to lead me far from all past moorings ; that bomb was the read-

67

ing of a book, and that book was Morgan's "Ancient Society."

Now my life had been that of a reader, delicate health as a child had lead me to devour everything in the line of papers, books, periodicals that I could get hold of. From eighteen to twenty-one I had read on an average of 250 newspapers every month beside magazines and books, and from my adventure upon studious life in 1895 up to 1906 I had read 1,160 books that I had made note of (an average of 105 a year) , and I had read in part and made note of some 800 more. In addition to this I had looked into and abandoned some hundred others, and had read as many papers and magazines as the average city editor of a daily paper.

Leaving aside my reading in political and religious matter before I was twenty-one, I had in the eleven years since that time, taken up one at a time and read into these topics; the Bible, with the historic and critical questions that center around it; theology; church history; philosophy; the history of religions; our civil war; spiritualism, and in addition I had been reading a good deal of history, literature and biography. And my study into these topics had not been superficial; I had read the best and biggest things. Such great books as Neander's "Church History," Von Oosterzee's "Theology" Mark Hopkin's "Outline of Man," Kant's "Critique of the Pure Reason," "Rousseau's Confessions," "Franklin's Autobiography," Bowne's "Philosophical Works," Henry George's "Progress and Poverty," "Altgeld's Speeches," Loyd's "Wealth vs. Commonwealth," Ameil's "Journal," these were some of the pets of my library, gathered after a careful reading of the best and profoundest books I could find on the topics mentioned above.

I do not feel then that I was entirely ignorant before I came to Morgan, and yet I did not know anything. I had a vast storehouse of facts, of knowledge and theory, but I did not have any key to unlock it, it floated about in my skull, so much unpacked cargo. In the summer of 1906 my minister's association gave me the assignment of a paper on "Divorce" for the February (1907) meeting. Early in December, 1906, I got after my reading in preparation. Observation had already shown me that this question of increased divorce was an industrial and economic problem, thrust upon us by woman's changed industrial and economic status. In looking thoughtfully into the New

Testament I saw that there was no warrant for the position in regard to Jesus' teachings that the churches usually take. Thus it was that I felt the need of careful preparation for my paper, and I was ripe for the revelation about to come to me.

The third book I read in preparation for my paper was Morgan's "Ancient Society." I began it just before dinner, and did not leave it till next day when I was thru with it. I turned and re-read parts of it. I got up and went out to walk and think it over. I went to bed and thought it over. And the more I considered it the more enthused I became. Here I had the most original and greatest piece of scholarship ever put up by an American, and it caused scales to drop from my eyes, it produced a revolution in my mind. In one great vision it enabled me to gather up the floating cargo in the hold of my skull and to pack it away in proper places.

I saw the economic foundations of human life, and it unlocked what had been to me a thousand mysteries. I could see where the great books in my library had led their authors astray, led me astray, where they had departed from facts and launched away on long, speculative excursions. Of course, I do not mean to say that the grasp of economic interpretations makes us to know everything, but I do now say that without it we can't know much. I now saw that the early Bible tales were simply Hebrew folk lore; I saw the narrow cell of tlie speculative philosopher and theologian. I saw the absurdities to be found in the histories. I had to dig down, to recast my whole mental outlook, and so in the forthcoming fifteen months I read 210 books.

I canvassed once more the realms of economics, politics, history, Jesus and theology. In doing this I had access to the good Haverhill Library, the Andover Theological Library, the Boston theological and public libraries and the private library of Levi M. Powers, the Universalist minister in Haverhill ; Dr. Powers having one of the best selected and stocked collections of up-to-date books to be found anywhere.

My Socialism had up to this time been a sort of dumb consciousness. I knew its political program, I knew its economic doctrines, I knew, as a child of the working class, it was the only political force that stood for the welfare of the working class. I felt this, but with the acceptance of economic determinism, my reading took on a new light—I saw where Marx had found out the same profound truth as Morgan, and from it showed society was an evolution as Darwin showed the evolution of the physical being; tho Marx was looking at history as an economist rather than an anthropologist, as was Morgan. I saw where it came into the Socialist philosophy and gave it its profound meaning; and so I became a straight out and out Marxian Socialist. And I did not take this position until I had read once more the best literature of conventional anarchist, single tax and communist social theories.

But the revolution in my soul was not over, the recasting of my thought in regard to religious problems, arising out of the study made necessary by Morgan, was a revolution in itself; especially so in regard to Jesus, where I believe I got a better insight into what He really was and meant, then comes to the lot of most students of Him. In this seeking for a hold upon the newer and larger religious thought I must record my indebtedness to the help and influence of some of my fellow Congregational ministers in Haverhill and locality, men who were brilliant and fearless men in championing a saner religious view.

This year I was bound to have a vacation, even tho I could hire no house, and so I bought a couple of tents and went out under the little pines in a pasture for a month, and I came back, having like Thoreau experienced nature as some folks experience religion, and fully alive to that vast fund of happiness that lies in nature rapture. Tho I was an out and out Socialist and attended the meetings of the Comrades, there was a network of personal matters that made it impossible for me to at once join the club.

One of my parishioners was John Glennie, an honest and blunt Scotchman, and stubborn as the race usually are. Glennie was a tallow Tenderer, and tho beaten, threatened, cajoled and driven, he had refused to sell out or be beaten out by the trusts. He was interested in the Hisgen bill to secure justice for the smaller dealers and at his request I went with him to a hearing at the state house to speak for the bill. My remarks so pleased Mr. Hisgen and his friends that he had them printed and distributed, and when he ran for governor that fall asked me to come to the convention and second his nomination, which I did. I also spoke about the state with him in the campaign, and he ran up a vote for the Hearst ticket of 5,000 more than the regular state Democratic ticket. The next year I went to Chigago to the Hearst national convention and made the speech nominating Hisgen for President, and during the fall I spoke several times in the various New England states for the ticket. But with the close of the campaign I sent in my application to the Socialist local and took the position that was in accord with my innermost convictions.

During the winter of 1907-08 I had come under the spell of Walt Whitman: "Leaves of Grass" made a profounder impression upon me than any book save the New Testament, and with the aid of Dr. Power's library I was able to read practically all the Whitman stuff, both by him and about him. Thus having burned my bridges behind me by taking the social position of a Socialist, and having inwardly seen the vision of the "Good Gray Poet" which is really the vision of Jesus, Tolstoy and all the great rebels, I feel that I had found my way, I was ready to follow it, my soul was ready to hear and heed the call of Old Walt—

"Listen I will be honest with you,
    I do not offer the old smooth prizes, but offer
        rough new prizes;

"These are the days that must happen to you:
You shall not heap up what is called riches;
You shall scatter with lavish hand all that, you
    earn or achieve."

And to heed such a call, meant for me, what it has ever meant for those who have been able to receive it, that I must take to the "Open Road." However we have made such progress that they can no longer hang or burn the reformer—they can only seek to tarve him out, and ofttimes they fail in that.

CHAPTER VII

THE OPEN ROAD

"A foot and light-hearted, I take to the
    Open Road,
The long brown path before me, leading
    wherever I choose.
"Henceforth I whimper no more, I post-
    pone no more.
Strong and content I travel the Open
    Road
"From this hour freedom;
From this hour I loose myself of limits
    and imaginary lines.
Going where I list, my own master, total
    and absolute.
"I will scatter myself among men and
    women as I go;
I will toss the new roughness and glad-
    ness among them."

Walt Whitman.

"No form of writing gives so interesting a picture of one's time, as the autobiography." —Emerson.

CHAPTER VII

———

THE OPEN ROAD

———

ANUARY 8, 1909, I came up to my thirty-fifth birthday, conscious that in the preceding months I had found myself. Filled with the joy of intellectual pursuit, finding in intellectual resources and study relief from family cares, poor health, lack of material things, my life had grown increasingly busy, so busy that I had lost sight forever of thoughts of money, praise of men, professional advancement. My life had become busy with those activities which afford one constant enjoyment, just as Cowper found it years ago, when he said:

"How various his employments, whom the world
Calls idle; and who justly in return
Esteems that busy world an idler, too;
Family, books, a garden and a pen,
And Nature in her cultivated trim
Dressed to his taste, and inviting him abroad —
Can he want occupation who has these ?"

My bark had drifted out from the channels, to where I was indeed verily worthless to execute or administer those petty things, which make up the activities which the world calls life and achievement, and hero I am content to let it drift, I shall never pull back into the stream. To take a book and go out under the trees and read and brood and dream and think or to draw up by the fireside, this is life, life that the wranglers in the money-marts or professional tread-mill, never know. Just think of the place to which I had come; with Jesus of Nazareth I had come to know what religion really is; with Thoreau I had come to see what God gives us if we get out of doors; with MacCaulay I had come to see that it is better to be a poor man and love books, than to be a king and not know them; with Tolstoy I had come to see that the social question is the question of the age, and with the Socialists I had come to see the solution of the question, and knew the joy which is above all joys, that of possessing a great truth; with Ibsen I had come to care nothing even if my life stand a little apart, for he is strongest who stands alone; with Turgot I had come to see that the greatest satisfaction of life is that of literary study, and that a pen can contribute more to destroy the artificial evils of mankind, than can money or official position. Making money, framing laws, getting rich, promoting amusements, doing business, securing fame, these may do for plodding mortals, but those who catch the glimpse of life as Jesus, Whitman, Tolstoy, Marx, and the other great souls saw it, they have gone on beyond all these things.

And looking back over it, I can but see that life is after all such a strange conglomeration — a chain of accidents, at least so far as my personal will is concerned, pushed me on to all this. First, of course, was the accident that happened to my parents in my birth, for conceptions are hardly ever intentional, it was an accident then that I ever came to be. And then there was the accident of ancestral selection and environment, which together make me what I am by virtue of natural capacity and training. Then there were the personal accidents, breaks in health, loss of work, meeting new people, pushed this way and that, all of these combined to bring me up here, truly, after all, the margin of personal free will is small.

Nature, literature, religion. Socialism, domestic affections, these are the streams of my life. But I cannot be passive, I cannot sit in my house by the side of the road and see the men go by. I must holler at them, I must cry out to them, in other words I must be an agitator. Of course, I have to agitate because of my philosophy; because I have come to see the awful havoc that the present social system makes, I must cry out against it with all my voice; but beyond this I feel I was born with the spirit of protest. It manifested itself early; a boy of 12, I ground my teeth in rage when they killed the Haymarket men; my heroes have always been the great rebels, outcasts, pioneers—men like Moses, Isaiah, Jesus, Abelard, Rouseau, Shelley, Marx, Thoreau, Whitman, Tolstoy, Darrow. And this natural rebellious spirit is a mighty happy thing for a Socialist to have, for protesting against the things that are, is bound to cost us something, make us martyrs in a way, but we don't mind this as much if we have something of this naturally rebellious temperament.

Socialism is no longer the bugaboo it was a few years back, at least in theory; but Socialism in Haverhill is a thoroly understood class war. Originating in a class feeling between striking shoemakers on one hand, and the manufacturing interests and "solid substantial business men" on the other, Socialism had in 1898 become a practical struggle in Haverhill for political power.

In this struggle the Socialists did succeed in electing a Mayor and minority of the city government for two or three terms, and it was only by the hardest kind of fighting on the part of the ruling classes, in which there was effected a conjunction of the church, the rumsellers and political grafters, that the rising tide of Socialism had been beaten back. Thus it was that any encouragement offered to this Socialist body, after they had fought so hard to kill it, was a red flag in the eyes of the "respectable" people of Haverhill. So it came to pass that having joined the Socialist Club I read the writing on the wall that I better move on.

As soon as I began to cast about for a new ministerial location, I received unsolicited some offers, one at an advance of $700 in salary, over what I was receiving, if I would not meddle any more in Socialism; and I also soon noted that churches that did not pay $700, all told, would not give me a hearing unless I promised to drop Socialism.

But I could not see it that way, and I want here to record my appreciation of the local ministerial body of Haverhill ministers, they would not for a minute think of the suggestion of some narrow-minded laymen, that a Socialist had no place in the ministry, and so it was that December 1, 1909, I secured a little church out here in the hills of Massachusetts, where I minister to a little group of forty souls, have my living and my freedom. Looked at in the most cheerful light my last two years at Haverhill were very trying; diptheria went thru us, cares and sickness abounded, so it was with deep breaths of gratification that I unpacked my goods and started life anew, out here in the big hills. Ware was one of two or three small parishes between which I had to choose and the thing that turned me here was a scene at the depot the first time I took a train from the Ware depot. Ware proper has some 8,000 people, mostly overworked and underpaid Poles and French. Times were hard here in the fall of 1909, that morning some Polish were returning to Poland, two or three weeping women were at the depot bidding these people good-by, they held up their babies to be kissed. When I came to decide where to move to from Haverhill, I could not forget those poor little women in black; heavy-faced, thick-lipped, dull-looking and homely, I saw them as representatives of the class that has borne the burdens of the world for countless generations, and I saw that Ware was my field. I thought perhaps I might teach a kindlier feeling toward these poor foreign people, might perhaps do something to help their lot in life, and so I packed up my goods and sent them on to Ware.

I came on here as a proletarian. Socialist preacher. That is, I elected to stay with the class into which I was born, the workers; as a Socialist, conditions were such as to forbid me from giving up my profession for active party work; as a preacher, I had gone back over the heads of centuries of ecclesiasticism to the very teaching and spirit of Jesus and the Apostles, and thus my message was strange and unrecognizable in the churches. So I could not look ahead to any special achievement anywhere, the lot before me seemed to be, to hold this sort of mediating position, and to do the best I could in a general all-around way.